So you <u>really</u> want to learn

Junior Maths

Book 3

Answer Book

GALORE PARK

So you really want to learn

Junior Maths

Book 3

Answer Book

David Hillard

Series Editor: Louise Martine

www.galorepark.co.uk

Published by Galore Park Publishing Ltd,
19/21 Sayers Lane, Tenterden, Kent TN30 6BW

www.galorepark.co.uk

Typography and layout by Typetechnique, London W1
Technical drawings by Ian Moores

Printed by Charlesworth Press, Wakefield

ISBN: 978 1 905735 29 7

First published 2009, reprinted 2010, 2012

The textbook to accompany these answers is available from www.galorepark.co.uk

Details of other Galore Park publications are available at www.galorepark.co.uk

ISEB Revision Guides, publications and examination papers may also be obtained
from Galore Park.

Preface

This book provides a complete set of answers to *So you really want to learn Junior Maths Book 3*.

Contents

Chapter 1: Introducing investigations

Exercise 1.1: Investigating number patterns

1. (a) Add 2
   (b) Multiply by 3
   (c) Multiply by 2, add 3
   (d) Multiply by 3, subtract 1
   (e) Multiply by 4, add 1
   (f) Multiply by 2, subtract 2

2. (a) $a = 10$ (d) $g = 44$
        $b = 15$ $h = 20$
   (b) $c = 21$ (e) $i = 41$
        $d = 12$ $j = 25$
   (c) $e = 21$ (f) $k = 30$
        $f = 25$ $l = 50$

Exercise 1.2: Investigating shape patterns

1. (a)

Pattern 4   Pattern 5

(b)

Pattern number	Number of horizontal lines	Number of vertical lines	Total number of lines
1	1	2	3
2	2	3	5
3	3	4	7
4	4	5	9
5	5	6	11

(c) 19 horizontal lines (pattern number)

(d) 39 vertical lines (38 + 1)

(e) 83 lines (41 + 42)

(f) 70

(g) 50

(h) 72

2. (a)

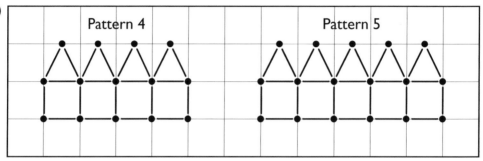

(b)

Pattern number	Number of lines	Number of dots
1	6	5
2	11	8
3	16	11
4	21	14
5	26	17

(c) 51 lines ((5 × 10) + 1)

(d) 38 dots ((3 × 12) + 2)

(e) 20 ((101 − 1) ÷ 5)

(f) 49 ((149 − 2) ÷ 3)

Chapter 2: The calculator

Exercise 2.1: Integers and decimals

1. 229
2. 44
3. 208
4. 35
5. ⁻71

6. 19
7. 2184
8. 15
9. 519
10. 13

11. 16.26
12. 13.74
13. 10.71
14. 80.5
15. 46.7

16. 36.4
17. 3.6624
18. 100
19. 141.84
20. 121.42

21. 1115.2
22. 7.808
23. 17.81
24. 29.73
25. 48.6

Exercise 2.2: Money

1. £4.48
2. £1.87
3. £16.50
4. £7.50
5. £4.13

6. £9.22
7. £1.34
8. £95.40
9. £2.05
10. £4.68

11. £2.50
12. £1.50
13. £19.33
14. £6.72
15. £14.80

16. £12.06
17. £1.45
18. £12.50
19. £1.25
20. £21.00

Exercise 2.3: Turning fractions into decimals

1.   (a) 0.6   (d) 0.475
     (b) 0.875   (e) 0.605
     (c) 0.6 recurring

2.   (a) $\frac{3}{20}$ $\frac{4}{25}$ $\frac{9}{50}$

     (b) $\frac{9}{32}$ $\frac{5}{16}$ $\frac{13}{40}$

     (c) $\frac{49}{200}$ $\frac{123}{500}$ $\frac{1}{4}$

     (d) $\frac{2}{5}$ $\frac{33}{80}$ $\frac{21}{50}$

     (e) $\frac{29}{40}$ $\frac{3}{4}$ $\frac{7}{9}$

Exercise 2.4: Brackets

1. 30
2. 22
3. $^-18$
4. 12
5. 19.8

6. 5.4
7. 31.5
8. 4
9. 36.7
10. 54.18

11. 0.575
12. 1.75
13. $^-0.9$
14. 101.5
15. 23.34

16. 21.64
17. 20.75
18. 5.25
19. 27.88
20. 38.4

Exercise 2.5: Approximation

Check pupils' answers.

Exercise 2.6: Checking answers

1. 47 643
2. 32 740
3. 28 314
4. 221 186
5. 307

6. 347
7. 469.4625
8. 64.3
9. 368.38
10. 42.5

Exercise 2.7: Problem solving

1. 44 547
2. £25 518.50
3. 150 000 apples
4. 31 536 000 seconds
5. 10 times
6. (a) 15 279   (b) 83 430   (c) 6697
7. (a) 29 463   (b) 869
8. 133 seconds
9. 15 seconds
10. £2750

End of chapter activity: Odds and evens

1.   6 − 4 = 2   E − E = E
        6 − 5 = 1   E − O = O
        5 − 2 = 3   O − E = O
        5 − 1 = 4   O − O = E

2.   (a) For example:

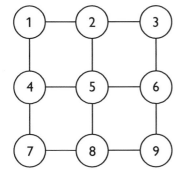

(b) Each pair contains 1 odd and 1 even number.

(c) The numbers can be arranged in different ways, as long as the even numbers are placed as shown.

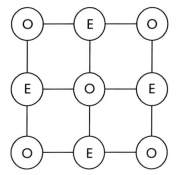

This will work for any group of nine numbers provided that five of the numbers are odd and four are even.

Chapter 3: Place value

Exercise 3.1: Writing large numbers in words

1. Four thousand, three hundred and twenty-six
2. One hundred and twenty-seven thousand, five hundred and three
3. Ninety-six thousand, four hundred and twenty-eight
4. Eleven thousand and eleven
5. Twenty thousand, four hundred
6. Three hundred and twenty thousand, one hundred and six
7. Fifteen thousand and five
8. Seven hundred thousand
9. One hundred and eight thousand, eight hundred and one
10. Nine thousand and fifty

Exercise 3.2: Writing large numbers in figures

1. 1456
2. 73 219
3. 148 607
4. 12 002
5. 7010
6. 284 600
7. 900 009
8. 600 000
9. 51 511
10. 27 000

Exercise 3.3: Place value and millions

1. 700 *or* seven hundred
2. 40 000 *or* forty thousand
3. 1 000 000 *or* one million
4. 9000 *or* nine thousand
5. 20 000 000 *or* twenty million
6. 400 000 000 *or* four hundred million
7. 60 000 000 *or* sixty million
8. 600 000 *or* six hundred thousand
9. 600 000 000 *or* six hundred million
10. 6 000 000 *or* six million

Exercise 3.4: Writing very large numbers in words

1. One million, two hundred and six thousand, four hundred and fifty
2. Two million, four hundred and fifty thousand and seventy
3. Twenty million, five hundred and twenty-five thousand
4. Thirteen million, thirteen thousand, one hundred and three
5. One hundred and twenty-five million, eighty thousand and seven
6. Four million, six hundred thousand

7. Forty-six thousand
8. Four hundred and sixty million
9. Four hundred and sixty thousand
10. Forty-six million

Exercise 3.5: Writing very large numbers in figures

1. 2 153 506
2. 67 110 654
3. 938 274 651
4. 6 000 000
5. 300 020

6. 30 500 000
7. 4 000 004
8. 60 006 060
9. 180 018 008
10. 1 001 010

End of chapter activity: Arithmogons

1. $9 = 6 + 2 + 1$
   $= 5 + 3 + 1$
   $= 4 + 3 + 2$

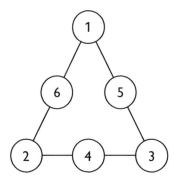

2. $10 = 6 + 3 + 1$
   $= 5 + 4 + 1$
   $= 5 + 3 + 2$

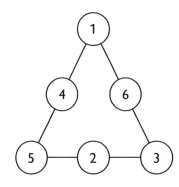

11 = 6 + 4 + 1
   = 6 + 3 + 2
   = 5 + 4 + 2

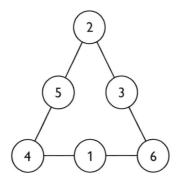

12 = 6 + 5 + 1
   = 6 + 4 + 2
   = 5 + 4 + 3

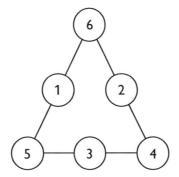

3. The numbers that appear twice in the additions must appear at the corners so that they are counted twice.

Chapter 4: Factors

Exercise 4.1: Divisibility by 2, 4 and 8

1.	34	116	70	
2.	56	68		
3.	96	160		
4.	128	2302	400	
5.	264	2484	3416	2008
6.	680	2784	3160	

Exercise 4.2: Divisibility by 5 and 10

1.	10	25	15
2.	30	60	10
3.	65	80	105
4.	120	200	

Exercise 4.3: Divisibility by 3, 6 and 9

1.	6	30	33
2.	12	18	30
3.	18	45	36
4.	42	57	84
5.	72		
6.	108	171	306

Exercise 4.4: Divisibility by 20, 25, 50 and 100

1.	40	60	100
2.	50	75	125
3.	100	150	200
4.	100	400	
5.	80	200	
6.	200	175	325
7.	400	250	
8.	400	800	2000

Exercise 4.5: Divisibility

1. 96
2. 100
3. 900
4. 198
5. 60
6. 129
7. 175 or 715
8. 600

Exercise 4.6: Pairs of factors

1.	1 × 12	2 × 6	3 × 4		
2.	1 × 16	2 × 8	4 × 4		
3.	1 × 18	2 × 9	3 × 6		
4.	1 × 20	2 × 10	4 × 5		
5.	1 × 24	2 × 12	3 × 8	4 × 6	
6.	1 × 32	2 × 16	4 × 8		
7.	1 × 36	2 × 18	3 × 12	4 × 9	6 × 6
8.	1 × 40	2 × 20	4 × 10	5 × 8	
9.	1 × 42	2 × 21	3 × 14	6 × 7	
10.	1 × 44	2 × 22	4 × 11		

11.	1 × 45	3 × 15	5 × 9			
12	1 × 48	2 × 24	3 × 16	4 × 12	6 × 8	
13.	1 × 50	2 × 25	5 × 10			
14.	1 × 56	2 × 28	4 × 14	7 × 8		
15.	1 × 60	2 × 30	3 × 20	4 × 15	5 × 12	6 × 10
16.	1 × 64	2 × 32	4 × 16	8 × 8		
17.	1 × 72	2 × 36	3 × 24	4 × 18	6 × 12	8 × 9
18.	1 × 80	2 × 40	4 × 20	5 × 16	8 × 10	
19.	1 × 96	2 × 48	3 × 32	4 × 24	6 × 16	8 × 12
20.	1 × 100	2 × 50	4 × 25	5 × 20	10 × 10	

Exercise 4.7: Square numbers and square roots

1 (a)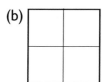

1 small square

(b)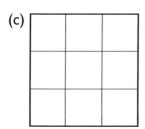

4 small squares

(c)

9 small squares

(d)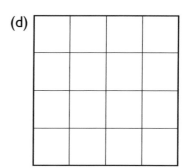

16 small squares

(e)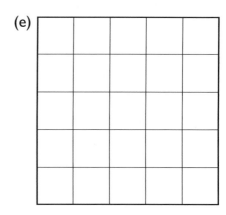

25 small squares

2. (a) 1
    (b) 2
    (c) 3
    (d) 4
    (e) 5

Exercise 4.8: Prime numbers

1. 13, 17, 19
2. 2, 3, 5, 7, 11, 13, 17, 19, 23, 29, 31, 37, 41, 43, 47, 53, 59, 61, 67, 71, 73, 79, 83, 89, 97

Exercise 4.9: Prime factors

1. 2 × 2 × 2 × 2
2. 2 × 3 × 3
3. 2 × 2 × 5
4. 3 × 3 × 3
5. 2 × 2 × 7

6. 2 × 3 × 5
7. 2 × 2 × 2 × 2 × 2
8. 2 × 2 × 3 × 3
9. 2 × 2 × 2 × 5
10. 2 × 3 × 7

11. 2 × 2 × 11
12. 3 × 3 × 5
13. 2 × 2 × 2 × 2 × 3
14. 2 × 3 × 3 × 3
15. 2 × 2 × 2 × 7

16. 2 × 2 × 3 × 5
17. 3 × 3 × 7
18. 2 × 2 × 2 × 2 × 2 × 2
19. 3 × 23
20. 2 × 2 × 2 × 3 × 3

Exercise 4.10: More prime factors

1. 2 × 2 × 2 × 2 × 5
2. 2 × 2 × 3 × 7
3. 2 × 3 × 3 × 5
4. 2 × 2 × 2 × 2 × 2 × 3
5. 2 × 2 × 5 × 5

6. 2 × 2 × 2 × 3 × 5
7. 2 × 2 × 3 × 11
8. 2 × 2 × 5 × 7
9. 2 × 2 × 2 × 2 × 3 × 3
10. 2 × 2 × 2 × 2 × 2 × 5

11. 2 × 2 × 3 × 3 × 5
12. 2 × 2 × 7 × 7
13. 3 × 3 × 5 × 5
14. 2 × 2 × 2 × 3 × 3 × 5
15. 3 × 3 × 7 × 7

16. 2 × 2 × 2 × 2 × 2 × 2 × 3 × 3
17. 3 × 3 × 3 × 3 × 3 × 3
18. 2 × 5 × 5 × 17
19. 2 × 2 × 2 × 5 × 5 × 5
20. 5 × 5 × 7 × 7

Exercise 4.11: Summary exercise

1. (a) 2   3   6
   (b) 2   3   6   9
   (c) 3   5   25
   (d) 5   10

2. (a) 1 × 36   2 × 18   3 × 12   4 × 9   6 × 6
   (b) 1 × 120   2 × 60   3 × 40   4 × 30   5 × 24
       6 × 20   8 × 15   10 × 12

3. 1   4   9   16   25

4. 8

5.   23   29   31   37

6.   (a) 2 × 2 × 3 × 5

   (b) 2 × 2 × 2 × 2 × 2 × 3

   (c) 3 × 3 × 3 × 7

7.   30

8.   22

9.   240

10.   260150

11.   (a) 12   (b) 21   (c) 4 or 9   (d) 4   (e) 17

12.   1

End of chapter activity: Magic dozens

Some examples:

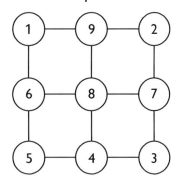

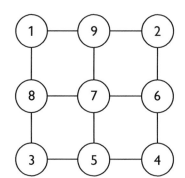

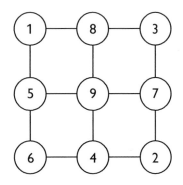

Chapter 5: Number properties

Exercise 5.1: Number properties

1. Check pupils' answers.
2. 12   13   14
3. Multiples of 3 (3 = 0 + 1 + 2, 6 = 1 + 2 + 3, 9 = 2 + 3 + 4, ... 48 = 15 + 16 + 17)
4. (a) 3 and 8   (d) 2 and 3
   (b) 6 and 9   (e) 9 and 10
   (c) 2 and 5   (f) 20 and 20
5. (a) 29 or 92   (d) 24 or 42
   (b) 45 or 54   (e) 18 or 81
   (c) 27 or 72   (f) 60
6. (a) 41 − 3 = 38
   (b) 38 − 19 = 19
   (c) 43 + 39 = 82
   (d) 33 + 87 = 120
7. 84×3
   63×4
   42×6
   36×7
   28×9
8.

	9 5 1	8 4 3	7 6 2
or	9 4 2	8 6 1	7 5 3
or	9 4 2	8 7	6 5 3 1
or	9 6	8 7	5 4 3 2 1
or	9 6	8 5 2	7 4 3 1
or	9 1 2 3	8 7	6 5 4

9. (a) 15 + 17 = 32
   (b) 38 − 34 = 4
10. 1 + 3 + 5 + 11
    or 1 + 3 + 7 + 9
11. (a) 51
    (b) 31
    (c) 49
    (d) 1

12. 1×36 2×18 3×12 4×9 6×6

13. $1 \times 1 \times 24$ $2 \times 2 \times 6$

$1 \times 2 \times 12$ $2 \times 3 \times 4$

$1 \times 3 \times 8$

$1 \times 4 \times 6$

14. (a) 3 and 4   (d) 55 and 56

(b) 7 and 8   (e) 314 and 315

(c) 24 and 25

15. (a) They are all multiples of 3. The middle term is the total divided by 3

(b) 456 $(151 + 152 + 153)$

618        $(205 + 206 + 207)$

789        $(262 + 263 + 264)$

3456 $(1151 + 1152 + 1153)$

16. (a) 40   (c) 27

(b) 55   (d) 24

17. 81

18. 64 (16×4) or 16 (4×4)

19. Even (the square of an even number is even)

20. Possible answers

$1 = 1$ $\qquad$ $11 = (4 \times 2) + 3$

$2 = 2$ $\qquad$ $12 = (4 \times 3)$

$3 = 3$ $\qquad$ $13 = (4 \times 3) + 1$

$4 = 4$ $\qquad$ $14 = (4 \times 3) + 2$

$5 = 4 + 1$ $\qquad$ $15 = (4 + 1) \times 3$

$6 = 4 + 2$ $\qquad$ $16 = (3 + 1) \times 4$

$7 = 4 + 3$ $\qquad$ $17 = [(4 + 1) \times 3] + 2$

$8 = 4 \times 2$ $\qquad$ $18 = [(3 + 1) \times 4] + 2$

$9 = (4 \times 2) + 1$ $\qquad$ $19 = [(2 + 3) \times 4] - 1$

$10 = (4 \times 2) + 2$ $\qquad$ $20 = (2 + 3) \times 4$

End of chapter activity: Similar sums

Each row, column and diagonal = 1 + 2 + 3
except for one diagonal which = 2 + 2 + 2

The total is always 3 × the middle number.

For 1, 2, 3

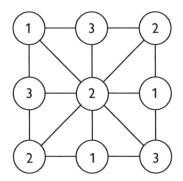   or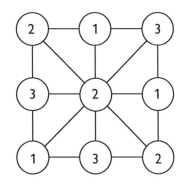

4, 5, 6 will give a total of 15 (5 × 3)

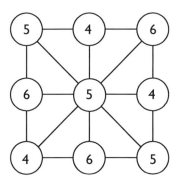

Any three consecutive numbers can be used.

Any three numbers can be used provided that the difference between the smallest number and the middle number is the same as the difference between the middle number and the largest number (i.e. the middle number is the median).

The total is 3 × the median.

For example:

14, 15, 16

total 15 × 3 = 45

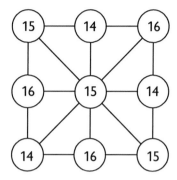

1, 6, 11

total 6 × 3 = 18

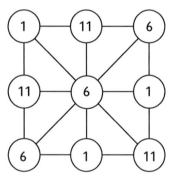

Chapter 6: Decimals, fractions and percentages

Exercise 6.1: Writing decimals as fractions

1. $\frac{1}{10}$

2. $\frac{9}{10}$

3. $\frac{2}{5}$

4. $\frac{1}{20}$

5. $\frac{31}{100}$

6. $\frac{4}{25}$

7. $\frac{3}{20}$

8. $\frac{23}{50}$

9. $\frac{1}{4}$

10. $\frac{1}{100}$

11. $\frac{9}{20}$

12. $\frac{1}{50}$

13. $\frac{13}{20}$

14. $\frac{1}{25}$

15. $\frac{41}{50}$

16. $\frac{22}{25}$

17. $\frac{17}{20}$

18. $\frac{18}{25}$

19. $6\frac{4}{5}$

20. $7\frac{9}{50}$

Exercise 6.2: Writing fractions as decimals

1. 0.9
2. 0.4
3. 0.17
4. 0.18
5. 0.15

6. 0.16
7. 0.25
8. 0.6
9. 0.7
10. 0.95

11. 0.5
12. 0.82
13. 0.84
14. 0.2
15. 0.85

16. 0.08
17. 1.1
18. 2.01
19. 5.72
20. 7.75

Exercise 6.3: Writing percentages as fractions

1. $\frac{1}{2}$
2. $\frac{1}{4}$
3. $\frac{3}{4}$
4. $\frac{4}{25}$
5. $\frac{1}{5}$

6. $\frac{1}{10}$
7. $\frac{7}{20}$
8. $\frac{17}{100}$
9. $\frac{2}{25}$
10. $\frac{4}{5}$

11. $\frac{13}{20}$
12. $\frac{7}{50}$
13. $\frac{6}{25}$
14. $\frac{18}{25}$
15. $\frac{1}{25}$

16. $\frac{2}{5}$
17. $\frac{21}{50}$
18. $\frac{11}{25}$
19. $\frac{9}{20}$
20. $\frac{1}{2}$

Exercise 6.4: Writing fractions as percentages

1. 13%
2. 22%
3. 36%
4. 35%
5. 10%

6. 80%
7. 25%
8. 50%
9. 46%
10. 20%

11. 5%
12. 70%
13. 48%
14. 75%
15. 78%

16. 72%
17. 85%
18. 60%
19. 6%
20. 12%

Exercise 6.5: Writing decimals as percentages

1. 47%
2. 36%
3. 89%
4. 60%
5. 6%

6. 81%
7. 18%
8. 50%
9. 55%
10. 5%

Exercise 6.6: Writing percentages as decimals

1. 0.48
2. 0.65
3. 0.5
4. 0.05
5. 0.19

6. 0.08
7. 0.8
8. 0.25
9. 0.11
10. 0.01

Exercise 6.7: Summary exercise

Fraction	Decimal	Percentage
$\frac{37}{100}$	0.37	37%
$\frac{71}{100}$	0.71	71%
$\frac{43}{100}$	0.43	43%
$\frac{1}{4}$	0.25	25%
$\frac{3}{4}$	0.75	75%
$\frac{1}{2}$	0.5	50%
$\frac{7}{10}$	0.7	70%
$\frac{3}{10}$	0.3	30%
$\frac{9}{10}$	0.9	90%
$\frac{1}{5}$	0.2	20%
$\frac{2}{5}$	0.4	40%
$\frac{4}{5}$	0.8	80%

Exercise 6.7: Summary exercise (continued)

Fraction	Decimal	Percentage
$\frac{11}{50}$	0.22	22%
$\frac{21}{50}$	0.42	42%
$\frac{9}{50}$	0.18	18%
$\frac{4}{25}$	0.16	16%
$\frac{11}{25}$	0.44	44%
$\frac{9}{25}$	0.36	36%
$\frac{9}{20}$	0.45	45%
$\frac{7}{20}$	0.35	35%
$\frac{13}{20}$	0.65	65%

Exercise 6.8: Problem solving

1. (a) $\frac{4}{5}$ (b) $\frac{7}{20}$ (c) 0.31   (d) $\frac{7}{10}$ (e) 0.69

2. (a) $\frac{1}{5}$ (b) 90%   (c) 50%   (d) $\frac{3}{20}$ (e) 0.7

3. (a) 0.23   24% $\frac{1}{4}$

   (b) 0.6   61% $\frac{31}{50}$

   (c) 30%   0.31 $\frac{8}{25}$

4. (a) 0.3 $\frac{1}{20}$ 4%

   (b) 72% $\frac{7}{10}$ 0.68

   (c) 16% $\frac{3}{20}$ 0.14

5. Samira
6. Tutus
7. 65%

8. 17 marks

9. $\frac{1}{5}$

10. Anne

End of chapter activity: Magic 15

(9 5 1)	(8 4 3)	(7 6 2)
(9 4 2)	(8 6 1)	(7 5 3)
(9 4 2)	(8 7)	(6 5 3 1)
(9 6)	(8 7)	(5 4 3 2 1)
(9 6)	(8 5 2)	(7 4 3 1)
(9 1 2 3)	(8 7)	(6 5 4)

Chapter 7: Fractions of quantities

Exercise 7.1: Finding a fraction of a quantity: one part of a whole

1. 12
2. 14
3. 9
4. 15
5. 15

6. 13
7. 13
8. 12
9. 54
10. 70

11. 18 marks
12. 6 plums
13. 18 red balloons
14. 17 customers
15. 16 packets

16. 20 yachts
17. 15 cakes
18. 16 white marbles
19. 150 exams
20. 309 children

Exercise 7.2: Finding a fraction of a quantity: more than one part of a whole

1. 12
2. 15
3. 12
4. 35
5. 48

6. 27
7. 45
8. 28
9. 69
10. 74

11. 87
12. 160
13. 54
14. 68
15. 98

16. 250
17. 288
18. 126
19. 78
20. 150

21. 64 girls
22. 45 children
23. 117 trains
24. 10 matches
25. 24 cashews

26. 98 staff
27. 175 children
28. £141
29. 48 tins
30. 25 girls

Exercise 7.3: Writing one quantity as a fraction of another quantity (1)

1. $\frac{2}{3}$

2. $\frac{7}{10}$

3. $\frac{1}{2}$

4. $\frac{5}{12}$

5. $\frac{1}{5}$

6. $\frac{2}{5}$

7. $\frac{2}{7}$

8. $\frac{3}{5}$

9. $\frac{2}{3}$

10. $\frac{1}{4}$

11. $\frac{1}{3}$

12. $\frac{12}{25}$

13. $\frac{7}{10}$

14. $\frac{13}{20}$

15. $\frac{1}{7}$

16. $\frac{1}{4}$

17. $\frac{10}{17}$

18. $\frac{2}{5}$

19. $\frac{3}{8}$

20. $\frac{1}{5}$

Exercise 7.4: Writing one quantity as a fraction of another quantity (2)

1. $\frac{3}{10}$

2. $\frac{1}{20}$

3. $\frac{6}{25}$

4. $\frac{1}{5}$

5. $\frac{1}{4}$

6. $\frac{3}{5}$

7. $\frac{1}{2}$

8. $\frac{4}{5}$

9. $\frac{1}{5}$

10. $\frac{1}{2}$

11. $\frac{3}{5}$

12. $\frac{1}{4}$

13. $\frac{2}{5}$

14. $\frac{1}{20}$

15. $\frac{2}{3}$

16. $\frac{5}{12}$

17. $\frac{3}{4}$

18. $\frac{1}{5}$

19. $\frac{1}{2}$

20. $\frac{2}{3}$

21. $\frac{1}{5}$

22. $\frac{1}{4}$

23. $\frac{1}{5}$

24. $\frac{1}{10}$

25. $\frac{1}{4}$

26. $\frac{2}{25}$

27. $\frac{1}{5}$

28. $\frac{3}{50}$

29. $\frac{1}{8}$

30. $\frac{1}{30}$

Exercise 7.5: Summary exercise

1.
(a) 26
(b) 8
(c) 64
(d) 78
(e) 105
(f) 75
(g) 420
(h) 450
(i) 300
(j) 375

2.
(a) $\frac{2}{5}$
(b) $\frac{1}{4}$
(c) $\frac{1}{5}$
(d) $\frac{3}{5}$
(e) $\frac{4}{25}$
(f) $\frac{2}{5}$
(g) $\frac{9}{20}$
(h) $\frac{5}{6}$
(i) $\frac{1}{3}$
(j) $\frac{1}{5}$

End of chapter activity: Number neighbours

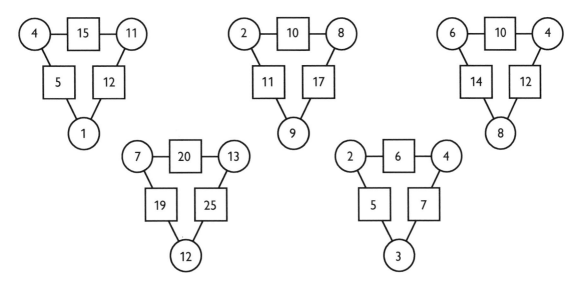

Chapter 8: Percentage

Exercise 8.1: One quantity as a percentage of another

1. (a) 70%
    (b) 34%
    (c) 92%
    (d) 80%
    (e) 60%
    (f) 5%
    (g) 60%
    (h) 54%
    (i) 40%
    (j) 24%

2. 40%

3. 45%

4. 20%

5. 25%

6. 39 out of 50

7. 45%

8. 40%

9. 10%

10. 82%

11. (a) 10%
    (b) 30%
    (c) 76%

12. 33%

13. 15%

14. 35%

15. 20%

Exercise 8.2: 50%, 25% and 75%

1. (a) 15
    (b) 62
    (c) £30
    (d) $125
    (e) 425 *ml*
    (f) £4.20
    (g) 68p
    (h) £2.50
    (i) $3.75
    (j) 4.5 cm

2. (a) 30
    (b) 12
    (c) £20
    (d) £9
    (e) 35 m
    (f) £1.15
    (g) £4.10
    (h) £1.50
    (i) 50p
    (j) 50 cm

3. (a) 18
    (b) 45
    (c) 150
    (d) £30
    (e) £450
    (f) £1.80
    (g) £3.45
    (h) £6.75
    (i) 6 m
    (j) 3.75 kg

Exercise 8.3: 10%

1. 6
2. 25
3. 4.6
4. 0.5
5. £60

6. 20 m
7. 90 g
8. £7
9. 4 kg
10. 8 *l*

11. £7.50
12. 28p
13. 63p
14. £1.25
15. $2.75

16. 4.5 kg
17. 1.5 cm
18. 9p
19. 5p
20. 35p

Exercise 8.4: Multiples of 10%

1. (a) 12   (b) £18   (c) 70p   (d) 80p
2. (a) 9   (b) £12   (c) £1.35   (d) £1.80
3. (a) 16   (b) £80   (c) 48p   (d) £3.20
4. (a) 48   (b) £90   (c) £5.10   (d) £5.40
5. (a) 35   (b) £56   (c) £1.68   (d) £7
6. (a) 56   (b) £96   (c) £1.44   (d) £2.40
7. (a) 135   (b) £270   (c) £1.08   (d) £4.50

Exercise 8.5: Fractions of 10%

1. (a) 2   (f) £2.10   (k) 19p
   (b) 9   (g) £6.40   (l) £1.08
   (c) 13   (h) 40p   (m) 20 kg
   (d) £3   (i) 25p   (n) 46 m
   (e) £1.50   (j) 12p   (o) 60 *l*

2. (a) 2   (e) £1.25   (i) 31p
   (b) 8   (f) 75p   (j) 50p
   (c) 7   (g) 4p
   (d) £3   (h) 12p

Exercise 8.6: Further percentages

1. 9
2. 14
3. 54
4. 77
5. 52

6. 17
7. 152
8. 13
9. £4.20
10. £20.40

11. £7.20
12. £14.85
13. £4.16
14. £2.70
15. 50p

Exercise 8.7: Value Added Tax (VAT)

1. £7
2. £49
3. £28
4. £24.50
5. £5.25

6. £6.30
7. £18.90
8. £11.20
9. 21p
10. 63p

11. £2.94
12. £8.54
13. £12.67
14. £16.03
15. £21.84

Exercise 8.8: Problem solving (1)

1. 60%
2. 18%
3. 20 marks
4. 150 g
5. 120 boys
6. 54 apples

7. £2.75
8. 27 chocolates
9. 200 balloons
10. 30 girls
11. £18.45
12. 10 tins

Exercise 8.9: Problem solving (2)

1. £48
2. £9
3. £272
4. (a) £40
   (b) £22
   (c) £7
   (d) 80p
5. £10.50

6. £285
7. £125
8. (a) £7
   (b) £52.50
   (c) £4.90
   (d) 28p

Exercise 8.10: Summary exercise

1. 35%
2. 44%
3. 6%
4. 35%
5. 30%

6. 18
7. £2.50
8. 17
9. £3
10. 30

11. 69
12. 25
13. 7
14. 3.2
15. 0.6

16. £12
17. £3.80
18. 60p
19. 7p
20. 3

21. £2
22. 25p
23. 3
24. £2
25. 60p

26. 36
27. 204
28. £77
29. £6.30
30. 54p

31. £3.12
32. 36
33. £18.20
34. £10.50
35. £6.30

36. 32 marks
37. 28 patients
38. 72 loaves
39. £16
40. £3.28
41. 26 biscuits
42. 75 g
43. 143 members
44. 40 books
45. (a) £63
    (b) £19.25
    (c) £4.20
    (d) £1.33

End of chapter activity: Number crosses

1.

		14				19				43	
	9	6	3		20	14	6		30	25	5
		8				5				18	
		16				23				41	
	10	7	3		40	6	34		26	14	12
		9				17				27	

2. The top and left-hand squares have the same difference as the bottom and right-hand squares.

   Example: In top left answer, 14 − 9 = 8 − 3

Chapter 9: Ratio and proportion

Exercise 9.1: Basic ratio

1. 1 : 2
2. 3 : 2
3. 3 : 1
4. 5 : 3
5. 2 : 5
6. 4 : 3
7. 4 : 5
8. 1 : 2
9. 3 : 2
10. 1 : 4
11. 2 : 1
12. 3 : 1

Exercise 9.2: Ratio problems

1. (a) 5 : 3
   (b) 3 : 5
2. (a) 7 : 2
   (b) 2 : 7
3. (a) 2 : 1
   (b) 1 : 2
4. 2 roses
5. (a) 5 : 4
   (b) 4 : 5
6. 7 : 3
7. 2 sunny days
8. 16 chickens
9. 2 : 15
10. 9 cashews
11. 3 : 5
12. 2 : 5
13. 10 : 9
14. 3 ice creams
15. 5 : 2
16. 4 sausages
17. 5 strawberries
18. (a) 4 red balloons
    (b) 2 blue balloons
19. (a) 2 : 3
    (b) 2 : 3 : 4
20. 5 : 9

Exercise 9.3: Multiples of ratios

1. 10 bottles of orangeade
2. 20 years old
3. 30 second class stamps
4. 1200 g (1.2 kg)
5. (a) 2400 *ml* (2.4 *l*) vegetable stock
   900 g leeks
   720 g potatoes
   (b) 360 g potatoes
6. (a) 675 g beef
   (b) 2 cans
7. (a) 2500 *ml* (2.5 *l*) squash
   (b) 1200 *ml* (1.2 *l*) concentrate
8. 50 minutes
9. 64 g strawberries
10. 60 pens
11. (a) 8 cm
    (b) 18 cm
12. (a) 250 g demerara sugar
    85 *ml* water
    25 g butter
    (b) 10 kg butterscotch

13. (a) 240 *ml* orange juice
    (b) 12 Palm Specials
14. (a) 10 packets
    (b) 1200 *ml* (1.2 *l*) sauce
15. (a) 30 children
    (b) 16 baguettes
16. (a) 625 g jar
    (b) 480 g cauliflower
17. (a) 1125 g (1.125 kg) potatoes
    525 g white fish
    450 *ml* milk
    (b) 16 people
18. (a) 2 rose bushes
    (b) 10 packets
19. (a) 8 gallons
    (b) 450 *l*
20. (a) 15 kg
    (b) 264 pounds

Exercise 9.4: Total of ratios

1. 44 chocolates
2. 44 members
3. 24 *l*
4. £100
5. 210 camels

Exercise 9.5: Proportion

1. $\frac{12}{17}$

2. $\frac{2}{9}$

3. $\frac{1}{3}$

4. $\frac{2}{5}$

5. $\frac{2}{5}$

6. $\frac{6}{7}$

7. $\frac{1}{4}$

8. $\frac{2}{7}$

9. $\frac{8}{9}$

10. 2 tins

Exercise 9.6: Summary exercise

1. (a) 3 : 2
   (b) 4 : 1
   (c) 2 : 1
   (d) 2 : 1
2. 9 : 4
3. 10 pots of honey
4. 60 A grades
5. 57 members
6. (a) 180 cm
   (b) 16 inches
7. (a) 3000 *ml* (3 *l*) vegetable stock
   1500 *ml* (1.5 *l*) milk
   1000 g (1 kg) mushrooms
   (b) 12 people
8. (a) 15 onions
   (b) 20 people

9. (a) 500 g Columbian
   (b) 600 g Mocha
10. (a) 300 g black pepper
    (b) 250 g
11. (a) 35 lorries
    (b) 336 cars

12. $\frac{2}{3}$

13. (a) (i) 4 : 7   (ii) $\frac{4}{11}$
    (b) (i) 21 letters   (ii) 33 letters

End of chapter activity: Tricky triangles

1. **Pattern 5**   **Pattern 6**   **Pattern 7**   **Pattern 8**

2.

Pattern number	Number of dots	Pattern number × next pattern number
1	1	$1 \times 2 = 2$
2	3	$2 \times 3 = 6$
3	6	$3 \times 4 = 12$
4	10	$4 \times 5 = 20$
5	15	$5 \times 6 = 30$
6	21	$6 \times 7 = 42$
7	28	$7 \times 8 = 56$
8	36	$8 \times 9 = 72$
9	45	$9 \times 10 = 90$
10	55	$10 \times 11 = 110$

3. (Number of dots) = (Pattern number × next number) ÷ 2
See the completed table above for the final two rows.

4. $15 = 1 + 2 + 3 + 4 + 5$
$21 = 1 + 2 + 3 + 4 + 5 + 6$
$28 = 1 + 2 + 3 + 4 + 5 + 6 + 7$
$36 = 1 + 2 + 3 + 4 + 5 + 6 + 7 + 8$
$45 = 1 + 2 + 3 + 4 + 5 + 6 + 7 + 8 + 9$
$55 = 1 + 2 + 3 + 4 + 5 + 6 + 7 + 8 + 9 + 10$

5. (a) 15th triangle number = $(15 \times 16) \div 2 = 120$
(b) sum of numbers 1 to 50 = $(50 \times 51) \div 2 = 1275$
(c) sum of numbers 1 to 100 = $(100 \times 101) \div 2 = 5050$
(d) sum of numbers 21 to 40 = sum of numbers 1 to 40 − sum of numbers 1 to 20
sum of numbers 1 to 40 = $(40 \times 41) \div 2 = 820$
sum of numbers 1 to 20 = $(20 \times 21) \div 2 = 210$
$820 - 210 = 610$

Chapter 10: Functions

Exercise 10.1: Finding outputs

1.	23	6.	30
2.	⁻3	7.	12
3.	72	8.	67
4.	4	9.	16
5.	5	10.	8

Exercise 10.2: Finding inputs

1.	17	6.	10
2.	27	7.	37
3.	1	8.	29
4.	100	9.	9
5.	18	10.	19

11.	7	16.	51
12.	102	17.	10
13.	10	18.	8
14.	18	19.	120
15.	47	20.	30

Exercise 10.3: Function puzzles

1.	7	6.	25
2.	5	7.	6
3.	13	8.	8
4.	9	9.	10
5.	12	10.	21

11.	32
12.	12
13.	22
14.	20
15.	23

End of chapter activity: Building bricks

1.

2.

Number of layers		Total number of bricks
1	1	1
2	1 + 3	4
3	1 + 3 + 5	9
4	1 + 3 + 5 + 7	16
5	1 + 3 + 5 + 7 + 9	25

3. (a) They are all consecutive odd numbers starting at 1
(b) Square numbers
(c) (i) 64 bricks (8^2)
   (ii) 900 bricks (30^2)
(d) 10 layers ($\sqrt{100}$)
(e) 14 layers in total ($\sqrt{196} = 14$), so 4 extra layers. 4 bricks are left over.

Chapter 11: Inequalities

Exercise 11.1: Inequalities

1. $10 > 6$
2. $30 > 29$
3. $6 < 8$
4. $4 < n$
5. $-2 < 0$

6. $n \leq 8$
7. $n \leq 0$
8. $n \geq 65$
9. $n \geq 5$
10. $n \geq 4$

Exercise 11.2: Finding largest and smallest whole number (integral) values

1. 8
2. 7
3. -6

4. -3
5. -1

6. 7
7. 10
8. -3

9. -4
10. 1

Exercise 11.3: Range of values

#					
1.	2	3	4		
2.	7	8	9		
3.	6	7	8		
4.	9				
5.	8	9			
6.	9	10			
7.	8	9	10		
8.	-3	-2			
9.	-3	-2	-1		
10.	-4	-3	-2		

#				
11.	-4	-3	-2	-1
12.	3	4	5	6
13.	-3	-2	-1	
14.	0	1		
15.	0	1	2	3	4

16.	10	9	8	7			
17.	8	7	6				
18.	3	2					
19.	8						
20.	8	7					
21.	9	8					
22.	9	8	7				
23.	4	3	2	1	0	⁻1	
24.	4	3	2	1	0	⁻1	⁻2
25.	5	4	3	2	1	0	⁻1
26.	5	4	3	2	1	0	⁻1	⁻2
27.	⁻2	⁻3					
28.	⁻5	⁻6	⁻7	⁻8			
29.	0	⁻1	⁻2				
30.	6	5	4	3	2	1	
31.	9	10	11				
32.	8	7	6	5			
33.	⁻3	⁻2					
34.	⁻7	⁻8					
35.	3	2	1	0			
36.	4						
37.	⁻6	⁻5	⁻4				
38.	0	⁻1	⁻2	⁻3	⁻4		
39.	⁻1	0	1				
40.	1	0	⁻1				

End of chapter activity: How many triangles?

1.

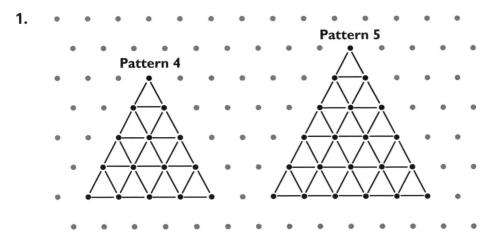

Pattern 4

Pattern 5

2.

Pattern number	Number of small triangles	Number of dots
1	1	3
2	4	6
3	9	10
4	16	15
5	25	21

3. (a) Square numbers
(b) Triangle numbers
(c) 45 dots (9th triangle number)
(d) 81 small triangles (9^2)
(e) Pattern 12 ($\sqrt{144}$)

Chapter 12: Decimal multiplication

Exercise 12.1: Multiplying by a single integer

1. 11.2
2. 8.4
3. 31.6
4. 43.5
5. 20.4

6. 1.47
7. 5.76
8. 7.47
9. 5.66
10. 23.88

11. 6.96
12. 19.85
13. 16.74
14. 130.2
15. 603.2

16. 447.3
17. 88.8
18. 225.2
19. 63.35
20. 212.4

Exercise 12.2: Multiplication of decimals by 10, 100 and 1000

1. 41.2
2. 356
3. 3560

4. 234.5
5. 4512
6. 12 340

7. 1231.5
8. 57 302
9. 482 200

Exercise 12.3: Multiplication of decimals by multiples of 10, 100 and 1000

1. 64
2. 282
3. 5.7
4. 227.5
5. 69.5

6. 43.6
7. 11.84
8. 2124
9. 882
10. 1.35

11. 3348
12. 438
13. 3715
14. 135.9
15. 78.3

16. 5880
17. 414
18. 9300
19. 57 200
20. 21 600

Exercise 12.4: Multiplying a decimal by a decimal

1. 3.12
2. 4.65
3. 3.75
4. 29.22
5. 4.806

6. 1.988
7. 6.064
8. 1.359
9. 0.64
10. 0.975

11. 0.915
12. 0.568
13. 0.96
14. 0.07
15. 0.0184

16 0.0084
17. 0.000 423
18. 3.35
19. 67.32
20. 0.2009

Exercise 12.5: Problem solving

1. £33.90
2. 13.3 m
3. 14 kg
4. 1.65 *l*
5. 37.42 points
6. 34.2 g
7. 12.7 cm
8. 5.68 m

9. 28.35 cm
10. £300
11. 10.75 g
12. £7.16
13. €4.04
14. 57%
15. 25.317 km

End of chapter activity: Chequered tiles (1)

1.

4 Tiles

2.

Number of tiles	Number of black squares	Number of white squares	Total number of squares
1	5	4	9
2	10	8	18
3	15	12	27
4	20	16	36
5	25	20	45

3. (a) 100 black squares (20 × 5)
(b) 96 white squares (24 × 4)
(c) 270 squares (30 × 9)
(d) 45 tiles (225 ÷ 5)
(e) 40 tiles (160 ÷ 4)
(f) 26 tiles (234 ÷ 9)
(g) 400 squares ((900 ÷ 9) × 4)

Chapter 13: Decimal division

Exercise 13.1: Dividing by a single integer

1. 2.9
2. 2.9
3. 2.3
4. 1.7
5. 1.3

6. 0.8
7. 0.9
8. 0.7
9. 8.3
10. 9.7

11. 8.4
12. 8.6
13. 8.6
14. 9.6
15. 4.7

16. 7.3
17. 8.6
18. 1.67
19. 1.68
20. 0.28

21. 1.19
22. 0.17
23. 0.02
24. 29.5
25. 15.7

26. 26.8
27. 12.6
28. 15.9
29. 24.4
30. 10.3

Exercise 13.2: Decimal division with a remainder

1. 2.65
2. 0.45
3. 1.52
4. 1.45
5. 2.15

6. 0.475
7. 7.35
8. 8.275
9. 4.78
10. 3.25

11. 0.495
12. 1.424
13. 1.05
14. 0.925
15. 0.015

16. 2.5
17. 3.5
18. 3.4
19. 0.375
20. 11.75

21. 4.5
22. 14.4
23. 2.5
24. 16.25
25. 3.875

Exercise 13.3: Dividing by multiples of 10, 100 and 1000

1. 8
2. 90
3. 7
4. 8
5. 3

6. 6
7. 24
8. 16
9. 44
10. 500

11. 7.2
12. 4.2
13. 6.4
14. 4.5
15. 8.7

16. 0.57
17. 2.4
18. 150
19. 60
20. 134

Exercise 13.4: Dividing by a decimal

1. 23
2. 17
3. 13
4. 19
5. 9

6. 17
7. 195
8. 7.7
9. 4.5
10. 4.3

11. 0.38
12. 39.47
13. 41.7
14. 59.1
15. 40.3

16. 3.15
17. 30.3
18. 1.19
19. 0.45
20. 0.076

21. 2.85
22. 2.25
23. 87.72
24. 6.575
25. 0.225

26. 215
27. 540
28. 245
29. 105
30. 334

End of chapter activity: Chequered tiles (2)

1.

Pattern 4

2.

Pattern number	Number of black squares	Number of white squares	Total number of squares
1	1	0	1
2	5	4	9
3	13	12	25
4	25	24	49
5	41	40	81

3. (a) 264 white squares (265 − 1)

(b) 313 black squares (312 + 1)

(c) 421 squares (consecutive numbers whose sum is 841)

Chapter 14: Long multiplication

Exercise 14.1: Multiplying using factors

1. 465
2. 1596
3. 1116
4. 1128
5. 1278

6. 2144
7. 725
8. 1162
9. 875
10. 816

11. 3024
12. 3942
13. 1656
14. 5355
15. 931

16. 2576
17. 1176
18. 1908
19. 1088
20. 1665

21. 5004
22. 18 865
23. 14 532
24. 5103
25. 14 706

26. 12 936
27. 25 024
28. 53 739
29. 14 496
30. 9936

Exercise 14.2: Informal multiplication by partition

1. 1209
2. 893
3. 851
4. 2457
5. 2691

6. 2592
7. 1026
8. 833
9. 1044
10. 5655

11. 9545
12. 21 862
13. 2244
14. 20 056
15. 31 098

16. 26 461
17. 14 363
18. 46 431
19. 58 007
20. 78 561

Exercise 14.3: Multiplying using the formal method

1. 1081
2. 3672
3. 5561
4. 3230
5. 1222

6. 2925
7. 4784
8. 5166
9. 2183
10. 1513

11. 4301
12. 29 889
13. 27 066
14. 18 538
15. 23 384

16. 43 596
17. 17 751
18. 27 645
19. 40 950
20. 20 329

Exercise 14.4: Problem solving

1. 1290 passengers
2. 1728 packets
3. 592 miles
4. 672 hours
5. 1344 labels

6. 988 seats
7. £9135
8. 6500 sheep
9. £5922
10. £69 336

End of chapter activity: Squares and crosses

1.

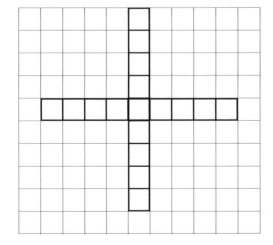

2.

Length of arms (units)	Area of cross (units²)	Length of perimeter (units)
1	5	12
2	9	20
3	13	28
4	17	36
5	21	44

3.   (a) 37 units² ((9 × 4) + 1)

(b) 84 units ((10 × 8) + 4)

(c) The length of the perimeter is 2 more than twice the area.

(d) 204 units ((101 × 2) + 2)

Chapter 15: Division using factors

Exercise 15.1: Dividing using factors

1. 15
2. 36
3. 52
4. 19
5. 57

6. 43
7. 29
8. 47
9. 23
10. 19

11. 76
12. 64
13. 86
14. 64
15. 69

16. 97
17. 37
18. 41
19. 34
20. 86

21. 123
22. 125
23. 186
24. 216
25. 341

26. 494
27. 614
28. 324
29. 561
30. 542

Exercise 15.2: Problem solving

1. 8 apples
2. 42 spaces
3. 23 chairs
4. 32 recruits
5. 23 km

6. 17 trays
7. £258
8. 54 box files
9. 75 bulbs
10. 38 drops

End of chapter activity: Dots and lines

1.

2.

Number of squares	Number of lines	Number of dots
1	4	4
2	8	7
3	12	10
4	16	13
5	20	16

3. (a) 80 lines (20 × 4)
    (b) 91 dots ((30 × 3) + 1)
    (c) 50 squares (200 ÷ 4)
    (d) 100 squares ((301 − 1) ÷ 3)

Chapter 16: Angles

Exercise 16.1: Measuring angles

1.	62°	7.	85°
2.	107°	8.	105°
3.	34°	9.	59°
4.	123°	10.	136°
5.	71°	11.	27°
6.	148°	12.	78°

Exercise 16.2: Drawing angles

Check pupils' answers.

Exercise 16.3: Angles on a straight line

1.	140°	6.	62°
2.	70°	7.	39°
3.	55°	8.	156°
4.	95°	9.	87°
5.	133°	10.	15°

Exercise 16.4: Angles

1.	$a = 120°$	6.	$f = 38°$
2.	$b = 45°$	7.	$g = 260°$
3.	$c = 147°$	8.	$h = 60°$
4.	$d = 23°$	9.	$i = 50°$
5.	$e = 40°$	10.	$j = 57°, k = 123°, l = 123°$

Exercise 16.5: The sum of the angles in a triangle

Check pupils' work.

Exercise 16.6: Angles and triangles

1. $a = 68°$
2. $b = 28°$
3. $c = 65°$
4. $d = 38°$
5. $e = 63°$
6. $f = 52°$
7. $g = 24°$
8. $h = 25°$
9. $i = 60°$
10. $j = 63°$

Exercise 16.7: Summary exercise

1. $a = 132°$
2. $b = 36°$
3. $c = 200°$
4. $d = 123°$
5. $e = 103°$
6. $f = 47°$
7. $g = 32°$
8. $h = 68°$
9. $i = 45°$
10. $j = 60°, k = 300°$

End of chapter activity: Equilateral triangles

1.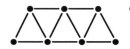

2.

Number of triangles	Number of dots	Number of lines
1	3	3
2	4	5
3	5	7
4	6	9
5	7	11

3. (a) 14 dots (12 + 2)
   (b) 41 lines ((20 × 2) + 1)
   (c) 71 triangles (73 − 2)
   (d) 60 triangles ((121 − 1) ÷ 2)

Chapter 17: Translation

Exercise 17.1: Reading translations

1. 6 squares left then 2 squares down.
2. 5 squares right then 4 squares up.
3. 7 squares right then 2 squares down.
4. 4 squares left then 5 squares up.
5. 4 squares left then 3 squares down.
6. 2 squares right then 3 squares down.
7. 5 squares right then 3 squares up.
8. 3 squares left then 5 squares up.

Exercise 17.2: Plotting translations

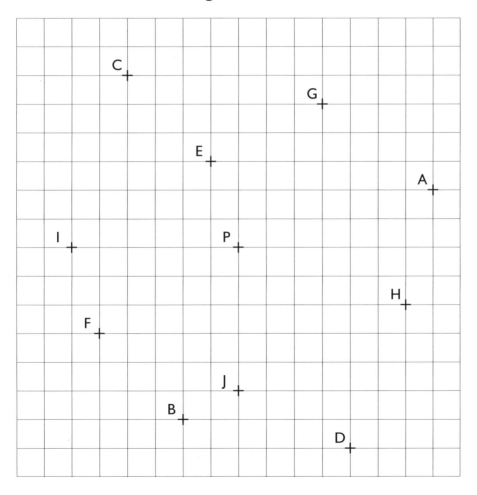

Exercise 17.3: Using a grid

1.   (a) 4 units left then 4 units up (−4 then +4).
     (b) 4 units right then 4 units down (+4 then −4).
     (c) 4 units left then 4 units down (−4 then −4).
     (d) 4 units right then 4 units up (+4 then +4).
     (e) 6 units right then 2 units down (+6 then −2).
     (f) 6 down (0 then −6).
     (g) 6 left (−6 then 0).
     (h) 8 units right then 2 units up (+8 then +2).
     (i) 2 units right then 6 units up (+2 then +6).
     (j) 2 units left then 2 units down (−2 then −2).

2.

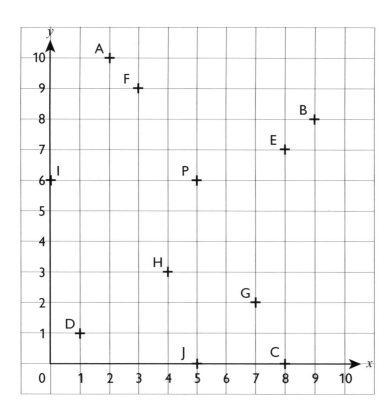

Exercise 17.4: Translation of shapes (1)

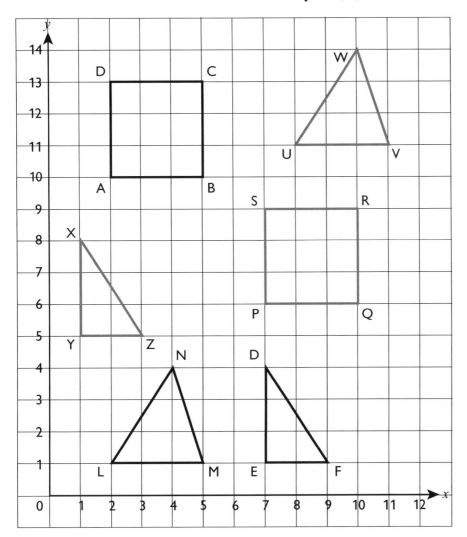

Exercise 17.5: Translation of shapes (2)

1. 8 units right then 8 units up (+8 then +8).
2. 3 units left then 4 units down (−3 then −4).
3. 3 units right then 1 unit down (+3 then −1).
4. 5 units left then 2 units up (−5 then +2).

End of chapter activity: Lots of L-shapes

1.

Pattern 4

2.

Pattern number	Number of squares	Length of perimeter (cm)
1	3	8 cm
2	5	12 cm
3	7	16 cm
4	9	20 cm

3.   (a) 31 squares ((15 × 2) + 1)
(b) 104 cm ((25 × 4) + 4) or ((25 + 1) × 4)
(c) 19 ((39 − 1) ÷ 2)
(d) 35 ((144 − 4) ÷ 4) or ((144 ÷ 4) − 1)

Chapter 18: Rotation

Exercise 18.1: Rotating a line

1.

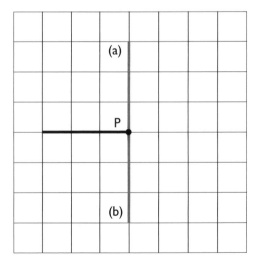

2.

3.

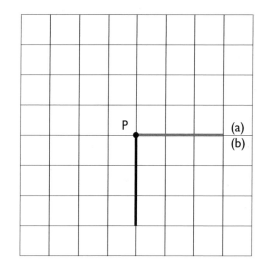

Rotations (a) and (b) give the same result.

4.

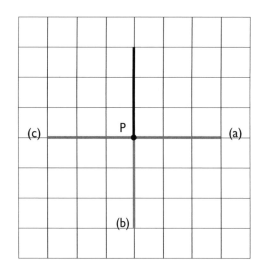

Exercise 18.2: Rotating a shape

1. (a) 90° clockwise
       (b) 180°

2. (a) 90° clockwise
       (b) 90° clockwise
       (c) 180°
       (d) 90° anticlockwise

3. (a)

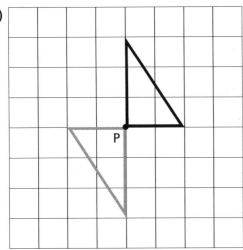

(b)

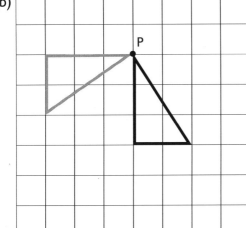

4. (a)

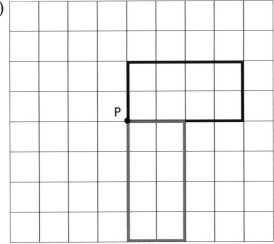

(b)

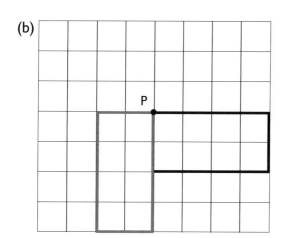

5. (a)

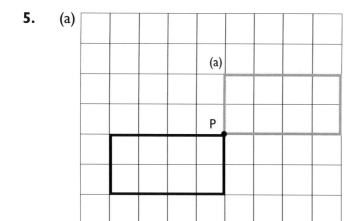

(b)

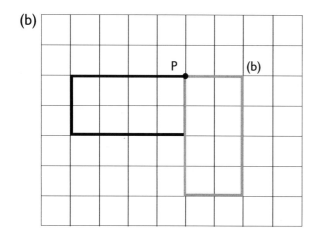

6. (a)

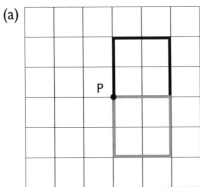

(b)

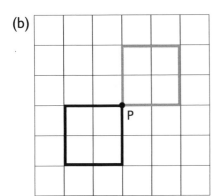

(c)

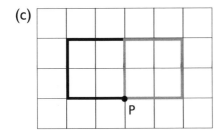

7.

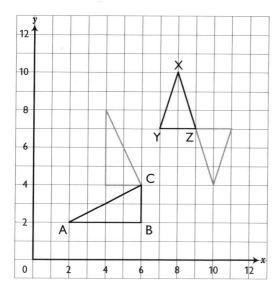

(b) (ii) XYZ is an isosceles triangle

See the above drawing for answers to parts (a) (i) and (ii), and (b) (i) and (iii).

8.

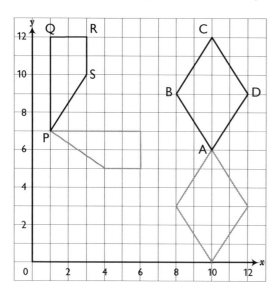

(b) (ii) ABCD is a rhombus

See the above drawing for answers to parts (a) (i) and (ii), and (b) (i) and (iii).

Exercise 18.3: Rotational symmetry

1.

Shape	Order of symmetry
Scalene triangle	None
Isosceles triangle	None
Equilateral triangle	3
Rectangle	2
Parallelogram	2
Square	4
Rhombus	2
Regular pentagon	5
Regular hexagon	6

2. (a) equilateral triangle, square, regular pentagon, regular hexagon
   (b) The order of rotational symmetry is the same as the number of sides of a regular figure.
   (c) (i) 10   (ii) 20

End of chapter activity: Find the numbers

$4A = 20$, so $A = 5$

$$2A + 2C = 22$$
$$A + C = 11$$
$$C = 11 - 5$$
$$\text{so } C = 6$$

$$2B + A + C = 17$$
$$2B = 17 - (6 + 5)$$
$$2B = 17 - 11$$
$$2B = 6$$
$$\text{so } B = 3$$

$$2B + 2C = 18$$
$$A + B + 2C = 20$$
$$A + 2B + C = 17$$
$$2A + 2B = 16$$
$$A + B + 2C = 20$$

Chapter 19: Area and perimeter

Exercise 19.1: Area of a rectangle

1.   (a) 54 cm²
    (b) 120 m²
    (c) 25.6 cm²

2.   (a) 35 cm²   (f) 8.6 m²
    (b) 108 cm²   (g) 17.4 m²
    (c) 60 m²   (h) 57 cm²
    (d) 300 cm²   (i) 123 cm²
    (e) 288 m²   (j) 10 cm²

Exercise 19.2: Finding the length and width of a rectangle

1.   (a) 3 m   (d) 7 cm
    (b) 6 cm   (e) 4 cm
    (c) 7 m

2.   (a) 7 m   (d) 18 cm
    (b) 29 m   (e) 37 cm
    (c) 25 m

Exercise 19.3: Composite shapes

1.   66 cm²
2.   50 cm²
3.   64 cm²
4.   55 m²
5.   26 m²
6.   48 m²

Exercise 19.4: Area of a square

1.   9 m²
2.   49 cm²
3.   81 m²
4.   121 cm²
5.   400 cm²

Exercise 19.5: Finding the side length of a square

1. 4 cm
2. 8 m
3. 2 m
4. 1 m
5. 10 cm

Exercise 19.6: Area of a right-angled triangle

1. 16 cm²
2. 30 cm²
3. 8 cm²
4. 9 cm²
5. 80 cm²

6. 10.5 cm²
7. 4.5 cm²
8. 22.5 cm²
9. 16.5 cm²
10. 24.5 cm²

Exercise 19.7: Perimeter

1. (a) 20 cm
   (b) 19 m
2. 100 cm
3. 5 cm

Exercise 19.8: Summary exercise

1. (a) 36 cm²
   (b) 50.4 m²
2. 49 cm²
3. 22 cm
4. 4 m
5. 24 m
6. 3 m
7. 22 m

8. (a) 5 cm
   (b) 25 cm²
9. (a) 70 cm²
   (b) 55 cm²
   (c) 72 cm²
   (d) 63 cm²
10. 4 cm

Exercise 19.9: Problem solving

1. (a) 150 cm²
   (b) 50 cm
   (c) 16 cm²
   (d) 134 cm²
   (e) 50 cm
2. (a) 20 m²
   (b) £700
3. (a) 320 m²
   (b) 11 packets, £14.52
4. (a) 120 m²
   (b) 7 m²
   (c) 73 m²
   (d) 46 m

5. (a) 620 m²
   (b) 110 m
6. (a) 176 cm
   (b) 640 cm²
7. 66 m
8. (a) 16 slabs
   (b) 10 slabs
   (c) 160 slabs
   (d) £240

End of chapter activity: A range of rectangles

1. 1 m × 9 m = 9 m² (area)
   2 m × 8 m = 16 m²
   3 m × 7 m = 21 m²
   4 m × 6 m = 24 m²
   5 m × 5 m = 25 m²
2. 1 m × 20 m = 20 m² : 21 m × 2 = 42 m (perimeter)
   2 m × 10 m = 20 m² : 12 m × 2 = 24 m
   4 m × 5 m = 20 m² : 9 m × 2 = 18 m
3. 25 m × 25 m = 625 m²
4. 1 m by 100 m; 202 m of rope

Chapter 20: 3D shapes

Exercise 20.1: Nets of cubes and cuboids

1. (a) Boxes in the shape of closed cuboids have six faces.
   (b) Most cardboard boxes in the shape of closed cuboids have three pairs of faces of equal size.
   (c) Check pupils' work.
2. Check pupils' nets.
3. For example:

(a)

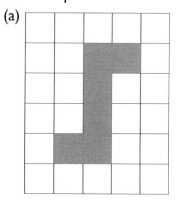

(b)

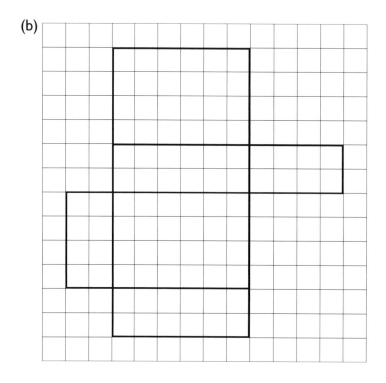

Exercise 20.2: Area with cubes and cuboids

1. (a) Check pupils' answers.
   (b) 96 cm²
2. (a) 6 faces
   (b) 64 cm²
   (c) 384 cm²
3. (a) 100 cm²
   (b) 10 cm
4. (a) Check pupils' answers.
   (b) 88 cm²
5. (a)   (b)   (c)   (e)   (f)   (h)   (j)
6. (a)   (c)   (d)

Exercise 20.3: Volume

1. (a) 60 cm³   (d) 640 cm³
   (b) 60 cm³   (e) 800 cm³
   (c) 280 cm³
2. (a) 64 cm³
   (b) 125 cm³
   (c) 1000 cm³
3. (a) 4 cm³   (d) 20 cm³
   (b) 10 cm³
   (c) 8 cm³
4. 36 cubes
5. 46 cubes
6. 5 cubes

Exercise 20.4: Problem solving

1. 3000 cm³
2. (a) 4620 cm³
   (b) 3465 cm³
3. (a) 96 000 cm³
   (b) 96 l
4. (a) 3456 cm³
   (b) Yes
5. 56 l
6. (a) 27 cm³
   (b) 18.9 g
7. (a) 54 bricks
   (b) 3 layers
8. 45 l

End of chapter activity: Perfect numbers

1. 28 (1 + 2 + 4 + 7 + 14 = 28)
2. 496 = 1 × 496
    2 × 248
    4 × 124
    8 × 62
    16 × 31
    1 + 2 + 4 + 8 + 16 + 31 + 62 + 124 + 248 = 496

Chapter 21: Line graphs

Exercise 21.1: Line graphs (1)

1. (a) 38.5 °C
    (b) 1.2 °C
    (c) 40 °C
    (d) Tuesday 8 pm to Wednesday 8 am
    (e) Mother didn't think it necessary because Ross was better, or she had measured a normal temperature since 8 pm on Thursday, or, perhaps, she forgot to take it!

2. (a) 450 mm
    (b) July and August
    (c) 150 mm
    (d) No. The rate of increase of rainfall is not constant.
    (e) The rainy season is beginning.

3.

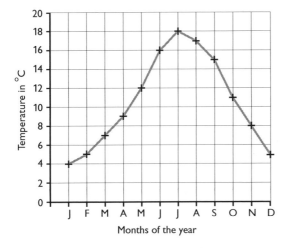

This graph has been reduced in size. Each square should measure 1 cm × 1 cm in pupils' answers.

4.

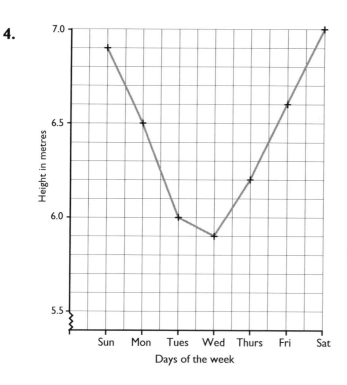

This graph has been reduced in size. Each square should measure 1 cm × 1 cm in pupils' answers.

Exercise 21.2: Line graphs (2)

1.   (a) £28
         (b) 2 hours
         (c) £4
         (d) £6 per hour

2. (a)

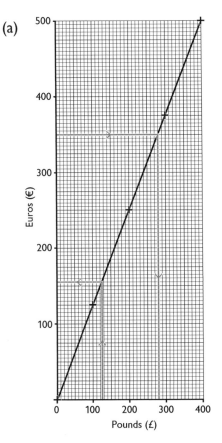

This graph has been reduced in size.
Each larger square should measure
1 cm × 1 cm in pupils' answers.

   (b) (i) £280
       (ii) €155

End of chapter activity: Two-digit numbers

1. 23 and 47   27 and 34   34 and 72
        23 and 74   27 and 43   37 and 42
        24 and 37   32 and 47   42 and 73
        24 and 73   32 and 74   43 and 72

2. (a) (i) 24 + 37 or 27 + 34 = 61
            (ii) 73 + 42 or 72 + 43 = 115
        (b) (i) 24 × 37 = 888
            (ii) 72 × 43 = 3096
        (c) (i) 42 − 37 = 5
            (ii) 74 − 23 = 51
        (d) (i) 23 ÷ 74 = 0.31
            (ii) 74 ÷ 23 = 3.22

Chapter 22: Arithmetic mean, range, mode and median

Exercise 22.1: The range and the mode

1. (a) 7
   (b) 5
2. (a) 6
   (b) 6
3. (a) 3
   (b) 1
4. (a) 7
   (b) 7
5. (a) 10
   (b) 12

6. (a) 9
   (b) 49
7. (a) 1.4
   (b) 7.2
8. (a) 0.3
   (b) 5.6
9. (a) 0.7
   (b) 1.8
10. (a) 0.6
    (b) 26.4

Exercise 22.2: The median

1. (a) 5
   (b) 42
   (c) 17
   (d) 16
   (e) 3.2
   (f) 12
   (g) 9.5
   (h) 98
   (i) 18
   (j) 36
   (k) 12
   (l) 1.5
2. 23 °C
3. 2.5 goals

Exercise 22.3: The mean

1. 6
2. 27
3. 120 m
4. 47 g
5. 2 people
6. 2 goals
7. 48 matches
8. 72

9. 6 cm
10. 82.5p
11. (a) 20 friends
    (b) 300 lengths
    (c) 15 lengths
12. (a) 40 members of staff
    (b) £160
    (c) £4

Exercise 22.4: Problem solving

1. (a) 1
   (b) 3
   (c) 3.3

2. (a) 49p
   (b) 10p
   (c) $7\frac{1}{2}$p
   (d) 10p

3. (a) 9 marks
   (b) 6 marks
   (c) 7 marks
   (d) 6.6 marks

4. (a) 4 children
   (b) 2 children
   (c) 2 children
   (d) 2.4 children

End of chapter activity: Piles of numbers

1. The sum of the numbers from 1 to 10 is 55. This total is an odd number and therefore cannot be halved.

2. Peter needs to discard one odd card, or add one odd card.

   For example, cards 1 to 10:

   1, 2, 3, 4, 5, 6, 7, 8, 9, 10

   Add another "1" card:

   1, 1, 2, 3, 4, 5, 6, 7, 8, 9, 10

   The new sum is 56, which Peter can divide evenly into two piles of 28, like this:

   1, 1, 2, 3, 4, 8, 9 and 5, 6, 7, 10

Chapter 23: Probability

Exercise 23.1: Probability

1. Certain (Christmas Day always falls on 25th December)
2. Impossible (Thursday always comes before Friday)
3. Certain (the sun always shines, although we may not always see it because of the weather)
4. Good chance (if the driver driving your school bus is usually a man)
5. Even chance (half of a pack of cards is red, and the other half is black)
6. Poor chance (the odds are 1 in 6 with a standard 6-sided die)
7. Good chance (if you are fit enough)
8. Impossible (Martians do not exist)
9. Good chance (if you have revised)
10. Only you know!

Exercise 23.2: Problem solving

1. $\frac{2}{7}$

2. $\frac{1}{6}$

3. $\frac{3}{7}$

4. (a) $\frac{3}{5}$

   (b) $\frac{2}{5}$

5. (a) $\frac{1}{12}$

   (b) $\frac{1}{4}$

   (c) $\frac{5}{12}$

6. (a) $\frac{1}{10}$

   (b) $\frac{1}{2}$

   (c) $\frac{1}{5}$

   (d) $\frac{2}{5}$

   (e) 0

7. (a) $\frac{1}{6}$

   (b) $\frac{1}{2}$

   (c) $\frac{1}{2}$

   (d) $\frac{2}{3}$

   (e) $\frac{1}{3}$

8. (a) 30 houses

(b) $\frac{1}{3}$

(c) $\frac{1}{2}$

(d) $\frac{8}{15}$

(e) 0

9. (a) $\frac{15}{22}$

(b) $\frac{1}{22}$

(c) $\frac{1}{11}$

(d) $\frac{10}{11}$

10. (a) (i) $\frac{4}{9}$

(ii) $\frac{5}{9}$

(iii) $\frac{7}{9}$

(b) $\frac{3}{17}$

End of chapter activity: Biscuits

There can be 3, 5 or 15 walkers, because there are a number of ways this could be calculated. Check pupils' answers.

For example:

2 plain biscuits + 1 chocolate biscuit cost 17 pence.
15 walkers × 17 pence = £2.55

or 6 plain biscuits + 3 chocolate biscuits cost 51 pence.
5 walkers × 51 pence = £2.55

or 10 plain biscuits + 5 chocolate biscuits cost 85 pence.
3 walkers × 85 pence = £2.55

or 19 plain biscuits + 1 chocolate biscuit = 85 pence
3 walkers × 85 pence = £2.55

Chapter 24: Mental strategies

Activity : Logical pets

Adam   : parrot
Bella   : cat
Connie   : mouse
Digby   : snake
Eve   : dog

Chapter 24: Mental strategies download

Please note that the answers below are for the complete version of **Chapter 24: Mental strategies**, available for download from www.galorepark.co.uk.

Exercise 24.1: Using addition strategies

1.	98	9.	176	17.	209	25.	580
2.	79	10.	169	18.	923	26.	598
3.	81	11.	142	19.	684	27.	602
4.	58	12.	112	20.	967	28.	752
5.	123	13.	170	21.	452	29.	600
6.	148	14.	156	22.	728	30.	902
7.	132	15.	92	23.	817		
8.	164	16.	312	24.	379		

Exercise 24.2: Doubling

1.	110	6.	161	11.	360	16.	550
2.	170	7.	176	12.	420	17.	920
3.	140	8.	134	13.	385	18.	730
4.	142	9.	53	14.	430	19.	756
5.	123	10.	145	15.	780	20.	1000

Exercise 24.3: Addition using a number line

1.	181	9.	156	17.	870	25.	170
2.	105	10.	163	18.	914	26.	600
3.	121	11.	246	19.	964	27.	272
4.	175	12.	574	20.	982	28.	898
5.	85	13.	342	21.	161	29.	950
6.	83	14.	430	22.	209	30.	825
7.	152	15.	729	23.	165		
8.	111	16.	900	24.	184		

Exercise 24.4: Subtracting by 'counting on'

1.	4	6.	5	11.	5	16.	7
2.	5	7.	5	12.	6	17.	9
3.	7	8.	5	13.	5	18.	9
4.	6	9.	7	14.	4	19.	8
5.	7	10.	11	15.	8	20.	7

Exercise 24.5: Subtraction with a number line (1)

1.	21	6.	46	11.	79	16.	232
2.	28	7.	44	12.	86	17.	185
3.	44	8.	78	13.	108	18.	252
4.	47	9.	117	14.	218	19.	183
5.	36	10.	151	15.	164	20.	511

Exercise 24.6: Subtracting by 'counting back'

1.	6	6.	8	11.	6	16.	12
2.	7	7.	8	12.	9	17.	14
3.	7	8.	11	13.	9	18.	9
4.	9	9.	7	14.	7	19.	8
5.	4	10.	9	15.	6	20.	8

Exercise 24.7: Subtraction with a number line (2)

1.	24	6.	32	11.	64	16.	26
2.	25	7.	25	12.	88	17.	73
3.	15	8.	21	13.	286	18.	445
4.	36	9.	24	14.	276	19.	397
5.	27	10.	33	15.	387	20.	504

Exercise 24.8: Multiplication by partition

1.	96	6.	280	11.	288	16.	1024
2.	102	7.	161	12.	966	17.	1462
3.	108	8.	153	13.	875	18.	1311
4.	315	9.	230	14.	928	19.	1178
5.	108	10.	348	15.	972	20.	2756

Exercise 24.9: Multiplying using factors

1.	216	6.	416	11.	2205	16.	966
2.	360	7.	912	12.	1325	17.	2220
3.	1050	8.	2240	13.	1494	18.	3456
4.	1080	9.	555	14.	1608	19.	1944
5.	308	10.	2016	15.	1520	20.	1512

Exercise 24.10: Multiplying using doubling

1. 156
2. 138
3. (a) (i) 45
       (ii) 90
       (iii) 180
       (iv) 360
       (v) 720
   (b) (i) 540
       (ii) 855

4. 1080
5. 1440
6. 1395
7. 1575

Exercise 24.11: Division

1.	7	**9.**	39	**17.**	30	**25.**	17
2.	45	**10.**	25	**18.**	50	**26.**	54
3.	6	**11.**	19	**19.**	46	**27.**	32
4.	70	**12.**	33	**20.**	16	**28.**	37
5.	12	**13.**	25	**21.**	19	**29.**	57
6.	22	**14.**	16	**22.**	14	**30.**	43
7.	48	**15.**	52	**23.**	15		
8.	45	**16.**	47	**24.**	14		

Notes

Notes

Notes

Notes

Notes